Essential Physical Science

MATERIALS

Richard and Louise Spilsbury

Raintree is an imprint of Capstone Global Library Limited, a company incorporated in England and Wales having its registered office at 7 Pilgrim Street, London, EC4V 6LB – Registered company number: 6695582

www.raintreepublishers.co.uk
myorders@raintreepublishers.co.uk

Edited by Andrew Farrow and Abby Colich
Designed by Cynthia Akiyoshi
Original illustrations © Capstone Global Library Ltd 2014
Illustrated by HL Studios
Picture research by Tracy Cummins
Originated by Capstone Global Library Ltd
Printed in China by China Translation and Printing Services

ISBN 978-1-4062-5994-0 (hardback)
17 16 15 14 13
10 9 8 7 6 5 4 3 2 1

ISBN 978-1-4062-6004-5 (paperback)
18 17 16 15 14
10 9 8 7 6 5 4 3 2 1

British Library Cataloguing in Publication Data
Spilsbury, Louise.
  Materials. -- (Essential physical science)
  1. Materials--Juvenile literature.
  I. Title II. Series III. Spilsbury, Richard, 1963-
  620.1'1-dc23
  ISBN-13: 9781406259940

Acknowledgements
We would like to thank the following for permission to reproduce photographs: Capstone Library: pp. 16 (Karon Dubke), 17 (Karon Dubke), 32 (Karon Dubke), 33 (Karon Dubke), 40 (Karon Dubke), 41 (Karon Dubke); Getty Images: pp. 4 (Adina Tovy/ Robert Harding), 11 (Monty Rakusen), 25 (Ryan McVay), 26 (NNE-CHRISTINE POUJOULAT/AFP), 31 (Jonathan Kirn), 39 (Peter Ginter); Photo Researches: pp. 7 (David Hay Jones / Science Source), 8 (Peter Bowater), 21 (Jeremy Walker), 30 left (Dante Fenolio); Shutterstock: pp. 5 (Harsanyi Andras), 9 (© design56), 10 (© demarcomedia), 12(© ppart), 14 (© Ruslan Kudrin), 15 (© Carly Rose Hennigan), 18 (© Tyler Olson), 20 (© TFoxFoto), 22 (© Pecold), 24 (© Ronald Sumners), 28 (© Matthew Racine), 30 right (© Ruslan Semichev), 36 (© Vadim Ratnikov), 37 (© John Leung), 42 (© EcoPrint), 43 (© Ales Liska); Superstock: pp. 13 (moodboard), 34 (Louie Psihoyos / Science Faction), 35 (Exactostock).

Cover photograph of a close up of colorful plastic chairs stacked reproduced with permission from Shutterstock (©V.Kuntsman).

Every effort has been made to contact copyright holders of material reproduced in this book. Any omissions will be rectified in subsequent printings if notice is given to the publisher.

Contents

Eureka moment!

Learn about important discoveries that have brought about further knowledge and understanding.

DID YOU KNOW?

Discover fascinating facts about materials.

WHAT'S NEXT?

Read about the latest research and advances in essential physical science.

Some words are shown in bold, **like this**. You can find out what they mean by looking in the glossary.

What are materials?

We depend on different materials every day. Materials are the substances such as metal and paper that we use to make things. They are used to construct cities, make homes comfortable, build computers and aeroplanes, produce foods and medicines, produce electricity, and to help us communicate, see, and hear. It is important to know about different materials so we know which ones to choose for different purposes.

Eureka!

In 2012 Chinese scientists discovered ancient clay pots in a cave in China. At 20,000 years old, they are the oldest in the world. The pots were probably used to cook foods such as rice.

A bridge can span a canyon or an ocean bay because it is made of tough metal and concrete that can carry the weight of cars and lorries. The pages of this book are made from paper because it is thin, light, and flexible.

This immense bridge under construction in Japan is made from many thick steel girders and concrete. These tough materials will keep it standing in the rough sea and supporting thousands of vehicles crossing it each day after completion.

Where are materials from?

Some materials we use are found naturally on Earth. Materials from living, growing things include wood and paper from trees, cotton and hemp from plants, and leather, feathers, and wool from animals. Non-living natural materials include rocks such as marble, sand, clay, and metals. Some of these are **raw materials** that we can use to get or make other useful materials. For example, we get useful metals including **iron** and **aluminium** from some rocks.

DID YOU KNOW?

The world's strongest material is called graphene. It is made from **carbon**, the same substance that pencil leads are made from. A thin sheet of graphene is 200 times stronger than a sheet of steel.

The tough leather suit and durable metal and plastic knee and elbow pads are materials that protect a motorcyclist from damaging his or her skin if he or she rubs against a road when travelling at speed.

How do we use materials?

Imagine a chair made from polystyrene or a concrete trampoline. The polystyrene would break when we sat on the chair and the trampoline would hurt us! We choose materials for things we make that have the right **properties**. These are features or abilities that help make objects useful.

Different properties

Materials can be hard or soft, strong or weak, waterproof or absorbent, heatproof or **flammable**, rigid or flexible, amongst other properties. For example, rubber and some plastics are flexible and can be squashed and stretched out of shape. They are ideal for making tyres, wetsuits, and hoses.

Eureka!

1839 Charles Goodyear accidentally dropped some liquid latex (a tree sap) onto his stove and it turned black and hardened into a tough but flexible material. He had discovered how to make rubber less sticky and so more useful.

Wood is a natural material that is strong, flexible, light for its size and can be cut easily into pieces. It can be used for many purposes such as those shown here.

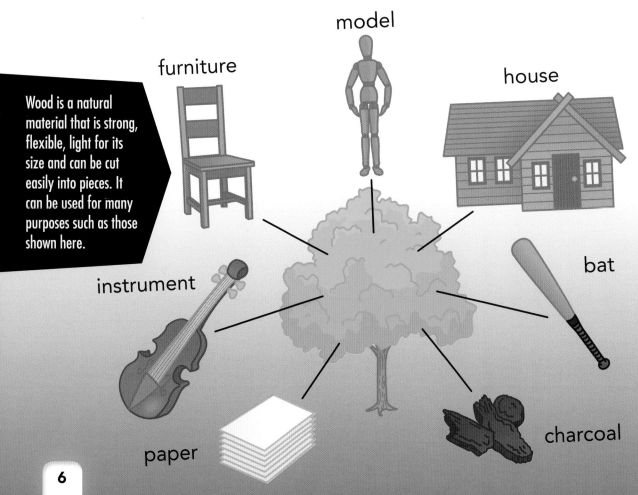

model

furniture

house

instrument

bat

paper

charcoal

Some materials can have some identical but some different properties affecting whether they are chosen for use or not. For example, glass and some plastics are transparent and good for making windows and clear containers. However, glass can break but is difficult to scratch whereas plastics scratch more easily but are more flexible. People make windows on aircraft from plastic because these vehicles shake and have to cope with strong winds as they move along.

Soil is an essential material for farmers to grow crops. It can also be used in construction as it is widely available, heavy, solid when packed and easy to shape when wetted to make mud, as here making the outer walls of this Earthship house in the USA.

Materials from underground

Some of the materials we need and use are found underground. These include coal, gas, and oil which can be used as raw materials to make other materials such as plastic. They are also our most important **fuels**. Fuels are substances rich in energy we can use for powering vehicles, heating buildings, and making electricity to operate machines. Materials found underground also include crystals such as diamonds and sapphires, whose properties of reflecting light or shining make them ideal for jewellery.

To reach useful materials near the surface people may use explosives to blast rock away and powerful water hoses to wash away soil. They may use powerful diggers or drilling equipment to reach materials deep underground.

The tall towers on this oil rig have long drills inside. These travel many kilometres underwater and underground to reach and pierce pockets of natural crude oil that then rise to the surface for use.

DID YOU KNOW?

The world's largest crystals were found in underground caves in Mexico and are over 10 metres (33ft) long. They are made of **gypsum**, which is a material used in plaster to make smooth walls and ceilings of rooms.

Used up

Some materials from the Earth are running out because no more of them are forming. These are **non-renewable** materials. For example, oil and gas are **fossil fuels** that formed underground over millions of years from ancient living things. People are using so much of these materials that there are only enough to last less than a century. **Renewable** materials can be replaced when they are used. For example, make a house from wood from a tree and you can grow another tree for making future houses.

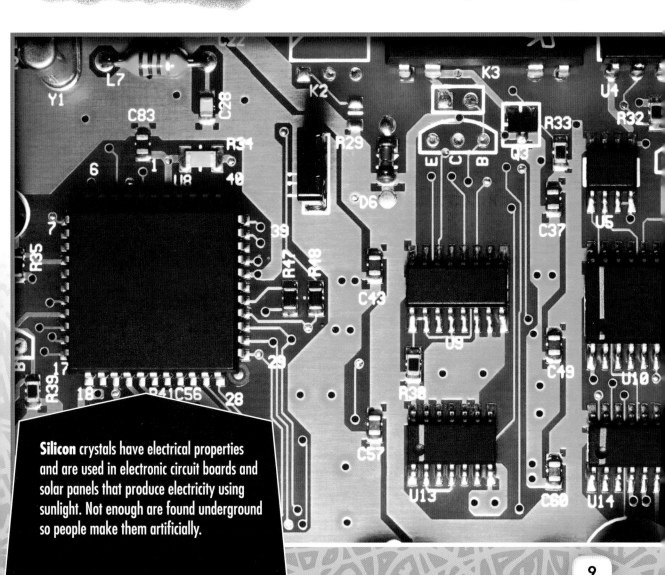

Silicon crystals have electrical properties and are used in electronic circuit boards and solar panels that produce electricity using sunlight. Not enough are found underground so people make them artificially.

Metals

Think of some metal objects that you may use regularly, such as saucepans, lifts, electrical wires, cars, trains, and even springs in a trampoline. Metals have many useful properties making them ideal for use in these objects. They are generally strong and hard. They are good **conductors**, which means that heat and electricity passes easily through them. Many metals melt only at high temperatures and can also be hammered into shape without breaking. They are also often reflective.

DID YOU KNOW?

You can bend some glasses frames made from the alloy nitinol out of shape, put them in warm water, and they unbend! That is because nitinol is a shape memory alloy that always changes back to its original shape when heated.

Fine wires in electronic devices such as computers are often made of **copper** metal because one of its properties is being especially good at conducting electricity.

Choosing properties

Not all metals have exactly the same properties. For example, aluminium is very light and easily moulded into shape. It is used to make food and drink packaging. **Alloys** are materials people make by melting and mixing metals with other substances with different properties. For example, adding carbon to iron makes steel, which is a tougher and harder material than pure iron.

The outer shell of a car or aeroplane is made from an alloy combining aluminium and metals such as copper. This makes it harder and protects the people inside better than pure aluminium.

Eureka!

In 1964 scientists developed a light material coated with a thin layer of metal that reflects heat. It was used to protect astronauts and spacecraft from overheating by the Sun's rays. Later, runners started to use space blankets made of this material to stop losing heat from their bodies after a race.

Plastics

Clingfilm, drink bottles, toys, mp3 players, and kayaks are just a few examples of objects made completely or partly from plastics. Plastics are materials people make with several general properties. They are waterproof, can be shaped using heat, are poor at conducting heat or electricity, and can be dyed to any colour. But people make and use different plastics for different purposes.

Eureka!

In 1964 scientist Stephanie Kwolek discovered Kevlar when she was researching new lightweight strong plastic fibres to replace steel for strengthening tyres. Using these fibres made tyres and therefore cars lighter. This helped them use less fuel.

For example, polystyrene (Styrofoam) is light and bulky because it is filled with bubbles of air. It is used for packaging to protect delicate objects from being damaged. Polycarbonate is stiff and tough and used for objects such as laptops, CDs, and sunglasses. PVC is also a tough plastic but is more flexible than polycarbonate, and used for anything from water pipes to window frames. Nylon is hard-wearing but soft and useful for objects including tights, fleeces, and parachutes.

The non-stick coatings to stop cooking food such as eggs from sticking to metal pans are layers of special heat-resistant plastics.

Layered plastics

Plastics are much lighter but usually weaker than metals. Kevlar is an example of a particularly tough plastic. Strong plastics such as Kevlar are made by weaving tough fibres into sheets that are then layered together using glue. Kevlar is used to make bulletproof vests, for example, and carbon fibre is used to make anything from fishing rods and tennis rackets to fast sports cars.

WHAT'S NEXT?

Scientists have developed plastics that can conduct electricity. In future there could be computers with no metal parts at all!

Nearly all tennis rackets today are made from different types of plastics reinforced with graphite fibres. This makes them tough, light and able to absorb vibrations when the ball hits the strings.

How do we tell materials apart?

Two pieces of metal, plastic, or wood can look almost identical but be different types of material. People can tell materials apart in different ways, including measuring and comparing certain properties that they have.

Colour

Some materials can be told apart by their distinctive colours. For example, crystals of sulphur are always a shade of yellow. Rubies are always a shade of red, from pink to the colour of blood. Other materials come in many different colours. For example, plastics can be made in any colour and sapphire crystals are often blue but can also be orange, pink, yellow, or green!

Many different types of gemstones are transparent, colourless and look the same, but others have distinctive colours.

Mass and size

A light grain of sand and a heavy boulder can be made of exactly the same material. Mass (weight) and size are not good properties for telling materials apart, but **density** is. Density is the mass of something for its size. Mass is measured in units such as kilograms per cubic metre. Most metals are denser than wood, but some are denser than others. For example, platinum is denser than aluminium and oak is denser than spruce.

DID YOU KNOW?

The densest material on Earth is a metal called osmium which is over 22 times denser than water and twice the density of lead. For example, a litre of osmium weighs 22 times more than a litre of milk.

People float logs by river from forests where they grow to cities where people want to use or sell wood. This can happen because the wood has a lower density than water.

Try this!

An object's ability to float, its **buoyancy**, depends on the density of the material it is made from but also its shape.

Prediction

Changing the shape of a material changes its buoyancy.

Equipment

- plasticine or other modelling clay
- aluminium foil
- scissors
- rolling pin
- 20-30 pennies
- large glass or clear plastic filled 2/3 high with water
- waterproof marker pen

Method

1 Cut a piece of aluminium foil around 30 cm (1 foot) square. Crunch it up into a ball. Then take a lump of clay and make it into a ball the size of the foil ball. Put them both into the water. Do they both sink?

2 Take out both balls of material. Use the rolling pin to roll the clay to about half the depth of your little finger. Carefully uncrumple and smooth out the foil with your fingers without ripping it.

3 Make a similar hollow boat shape out of the clay and the foil. Now put both of these on the water in the bowl. Do they both float?

4 Observe how deep in the water the clay boat is floating. Using your fingernail scratch a line showing the water level on the boat.

5 Put the boat back in the water and add 10 pennies, spread across the bottom of the boats. Where is the water level now?

6 Add more pennies to the boat. How many did it take to make it sink?

Results

The foil ball floats while the clay ball does not because the clay has a greater density. The clay sinks when it is formed into a boat shape. The density of the clay material has not changed but the density of the object has. The air the boat shape contains makes it less dense than water. Adding pennies to the clay boat increases its weight although it remains the same size. It sinks when its density is greater than that of water.

Hardness

A sponge can be squashed in our fingers but a piece of granite rock cannot. This is partly because the sponge has air spaces inside. It's also because the material it is made from is softer than the granite. We can test hardness in different ways. One way is to see if a material can be scratched by materials we know are hard, such as diamond. Diamond can scratch all other materials. It can be used, for example, on the edges of saws used to cut into hard rocks and metals. Natural diamonds are rare, so these tools use tiny pieces of diamonds cut into shapes with sharp edges.

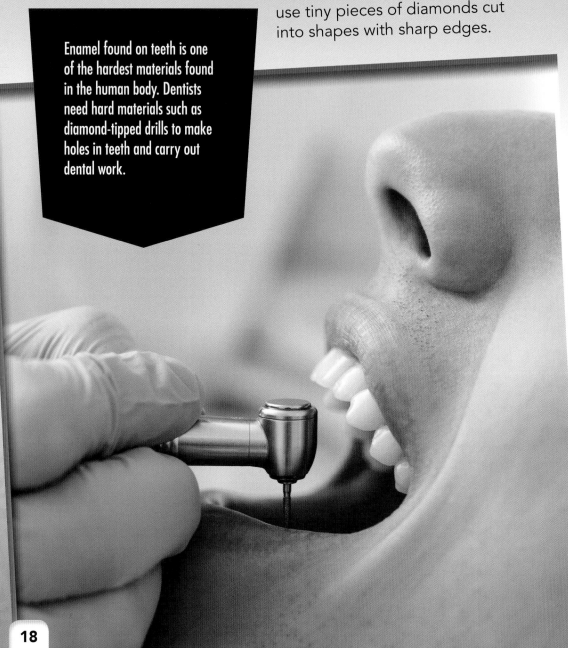

Enamel found on teeth is one of the hardest materials found in the human body. Dentists need hard materials such as diamond-tipped drills to make holes in teeth and carry out dental work.

Inside materials

Hardness and other properties of a material depend on what is inside. All matter is made up of tiny, invisible **atoms**. The atoms are held together by pulling forces called **bonds**. The bond strength and the arrangement of atoms varies between materials. For example, graphite used as pencil lead is soft and diamond is hard, yet both are made up of carbon atoms in different arrangements.

Eureka!

In 2005, scientists in California, USA, created a new superhard material called rhenium diboride that can scratch diamonds. It can be used instead of diamond in cutting machines, but is much cheaper to make.

Graphite

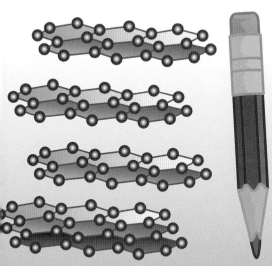

Diamond

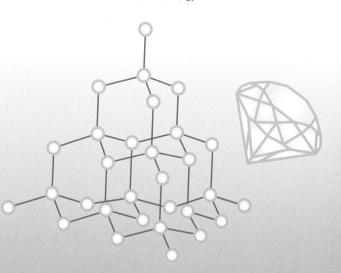

Diamond is hard because its atoms are bonded tightly with surrounding atoms. In graphite the carbon atoms are bonded in strong layers but these can easily slide past each other.

Conductors

Have you ever seen someone heating popcorn until it jumps around? Atoms are a bit like popcorn because they **vibrate** or jiggle around when they get hot! When one atom vibrates it can pass on heat to atoms around it which vibrate too. This is the way that heat spreads or **conducts** through the material.

We can test and compare materials by how well they conduct heat. Materials such as metals are good conductors of heat. Other materials such as plastics are **insulators** because they do not conduct heat well.

DID YOU KNOW?

Diamond is the best conductor of heat of all materials because its atoms pass on vibrations very easily.

The outermost layer of firefighters' suits are made of highly heatproof and tough material woven from PBI and Kevlar plastic fibres. These insulating materials are the first line of defence for the firefighter.

Magnetism

Another **property** of a material is whether it is attracted to or pulled towards a magnet. For example, we can pick up paperclips but not paper with a magnet. Magnetic materials include certain metals such as iron, nickel, and cobalt, and different alloys containing these metals. Most other materials and other metals such as aluminium and copper are not magnetic. The pulling force of magnetism is used in many ways, such as holding notes to a fridge and holding doors shut.

Eureka moment!

The first magnets used were natural stones called lodestones. The word "lode" means lead, and the property of this stone was discovered by Ancient Greeks over 2,000 years ago.

Magnets are used to separate objects made out of steel from mixtures of different materials in waste. The steel can be melted down and made into new objects.

How do materials change physically?

Put fruit and yoghurt in a blender and you make a smoothie. The same materials are still there but chopped into tiny pieces and mixed together. This is one example of a physical change. Materials can change physically by many different methods. People may use machines to cut, saw, grate, grind, or roll materials into smaller pieces or different shapes.

Rock changes

Materials can also change through natural processes. This is how solid rock can be worn away to form dramatic arches and other shapes. This is called **weathering** and can be caused by water, wind, and ice. You know how ice cubes take up more space than the water they formed from? In the same way, water in a rock crack freezes, swells, pushes the crack open, and breaks off rock. Broken pieces may be washed or blown away. This is **erosion**. Sandy beaches are places where eroded rock and also shells collect.

The magnificent arch in the desert in Utah, USA, formed over thousands of years as wind-blown sand gradually weathered the sandstone rock.

Over time new rock can form when weathered pieces are buried and pressed together. This type of rock is called sedimentary rock, such as sandstone and **limestone**. Sedimentary rock can change into metamorphic rock when heated and pressed deep underground. This is how limestone can become marble. Underground rock can get so hot that it melts. The melted rock can come out in volcanoes and then cool and harden into new igneous rock such as granite.

DID YOU KNOW?

Each year the Amazon River carries around 1 billion tonnes of weathered rock and soil into the Atlantic Ocean. That is enough to fill 200,000 Olympic sized swimming pools!

The rock cycle is how weathered and eroded rocks gradually change into new rocks. It is very slow and happens over millions of years.

Animal dies and is quickly covered with sediment.

Soft parts of animal (skin, muscle, etc.) rot away, leaving skeleton.

Minerals in bone change as rock forms.

After millions of years rock is eroded and fossil exposed at surface.

Changing state

One of the most obvious changes in any material is when it changes from a solid to a liquid or from a liquid to a gas. We call this sort of change a change of state. Particles in a solid are held closely together and arranged in a pattern. In a liquid the **molecules** are spaced out and flow past each other, but in a gas they move around in all directions and have no pattern. Warming or cooling an object can change the arrangement of molecules. That is why a solid ice cube melts into liquid water and a puddle of liquid water can turn into a gas in the air on a warm, sunny day.

Changes of state are **reversible**. For example, boiling water makes some of it **evaporate** and turn into a gas in the air. If that steam hits a cold window, it cools down again and turns back into liquid water on the glass. This is **condensation**.

Melting chocolate chips into a liquid and then letting it cool and harden into rabbit shapes in **moulds** involves two changes of state.

Temperatures of change

Materials have particular temperatures at which they change state called **melting**, **freezing**, and **boiling points**. For example, the boiling point of water is 100°C (212°F). People can use these tell-tale temperatures to identify materials. For example, the melting point of copper is 1083°C (1981°F) but that of pure gold is 1063°C (1946°F).

The atmospheric smoke behind this band at a live concert is actually from dry ice. The white clouds form when very cold solid carbon dioxide changes straight into a gas without going through a liquid state first.

DID YOU KNOW?

Carbon dioxide and iodine are two unusual materials that change from gas to solid and vice versa without a liquid state in between.

Mixtures

Seawater tastes salty because it is water with salt **dissolved** in it. It is a type of mixture of two different materials. We say that water is a **solvent** because it is the substance that does the dissolving and salt is a **solute** because it dissolves. Together, a solvent and solute form a **solution**.

One way to tell materials apart is whether they dissolve in water. For example, sugar does but oil does not. However, oil and other materials can dissolve in different solvents such as alcohol. Some materials may look like they have dissolved when they have not. For example, mixing soil and water makes thin mud. This type of mixture is called a suspension. But leave mud to stand and the denser soil sinks to the bottom, with water at the top.

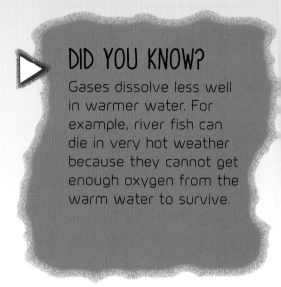

DID YOU KNOW?

Gases dissolve less well in warmer water. For example, river fish can die in very hot weather because they cannot get enough oxygen from the warm water to survive.

People who create perfumes blend scented oils together and then dissolve them in alcohol. This solvent mixes the oils together thoroughly and also evaporates quickly on skin, so the perfume can be smelled more easily.

Removing materials from mixtures

After cooking pasta in water we separate the solid from the liquid with a sieve. A solution cannot be separated like this. Instead it can be heated in a container to evaporate or turn the solvent into a gas leaving the solute. The gas can also be collected and condensed.

WHAT'S NEXT?

In future people may float strings of solar cucumbers at sea to make drinking water! Each "cucumber" is a box that uses heat from the sun to evaporate seawater to remove the salt from it. It also uses solar power to remove impurities from the water and then pump it ashore through pipes.

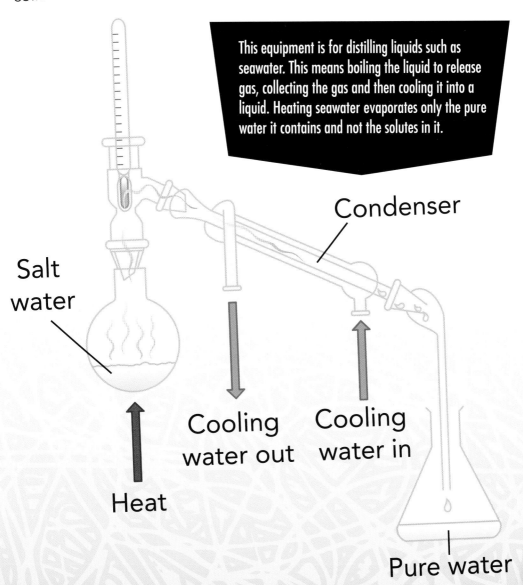

This equipment is for distilling liquids such as seawater. This means boiling the liquid to release gas, collecting the gas and then cooling it into a liquid. Heating seawater evaporates only the pure water it contains and not the solutes in it.

Condenser

Salt water

Cooling water out

Cooling water in

Heat

Pure water

What are chemical changes?

Have you ever watched a lit candle and seen it gradually get shorter? Heat from the flame melts the wax. This is a physical change. But then the liquid wax soaks up the wick and sets alight. The wax burns away. This is a type of **chemical reaction**.

During a chemical reaction, atoms join together in different ways to produce new materials. When candle wax burns, atoms in the wax join with oxygen atoms from the air. They make carbon dioxide and water vapour, and these gases escape into the air around the flame. The wax gradually disappears as it changes into these different materials.

DID YOU KNOW?

Important chemical reactions take place in your body each day. One is called respiration, which is when food reacts with oxygen that you breathe in, releasing energy to move and grow.

Rusting is a type of chemical reaction. In this reaction hard iron or steel combines with oxygen from air or water to make crumbly red iron oxide.

Permanent change

To make pancakes we mix together milk, eggs, and flour and cook the batter in a pan. It is impossible to take a pancake apart and change it back into the original ingredients. Like most chemical reactions, cooking pancakes is **irreversible**, which means it is permanent.

The honeycomb brick inside a catalytic converter contains special metals. These make harmful gases leaving the engine after fuel burns react. A chemical change makes harmless gases that leave the car through its exhaust.

Eureka!

In 1973 Carl Keith and John Mooney invented a catalytic converter. This device uses chemical reactions to clean harmful exhaust gases before they leave cars to reduce air pollution. This invention has been fitted to nearly a billion cars, reducing lung and throat diseases, and saving hundreds of thousands of lives.

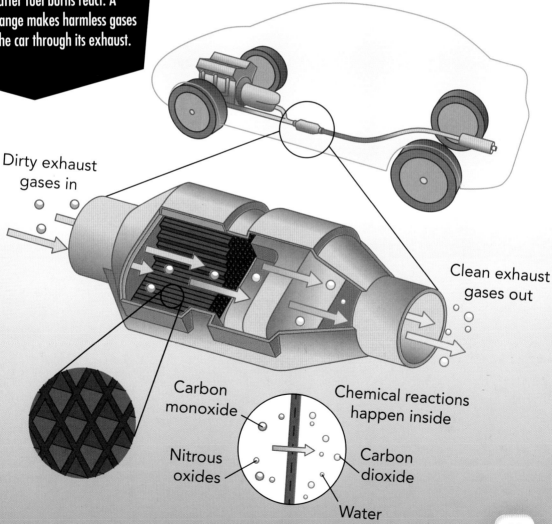

Dirty exhaust gases in

Clean exhaust gases out

Carbon monoxide

Nitrous oxides

Chemical reactions happen inside

Carbon dioxide

Water

Changes during reactions

Take a bite from an apple, leave it for an hour, and see how the fruit turns brown. This is because colourless chemicals in it have reacted with oxygen from air to make a brown chemical. This is a **product** of the reaction. Changes in colour are one sign that a chemical reaction has taken place and new products have formed. During some reactions gases are produced and this can be seen and heard as fizzing or bubbling when it happens in liquids. For example, one product of the reaction between bicarbonate of soda and vinegar is carbon dioxide gas.

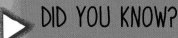

DID YOU KNOW?

Muddy estuaries smell of rotten eggs because of a chemical reaction in bacteria living there. The reaction releases energy from dead organisms in the mud that the bacteria need but one of the products of the reaction is smelly hydrogen sulfide gas.

The cockatoo squid lives in the dark depths of the oceans and uses chemical reactions to make light around its eyes to attract prey. Fireworks are explosive, colourful chemical reactions in the sky.

How does it react?

Put a piece of iron in water and the reaction is too slow to see. Put a piece of sodium metal in water and it reacts suddenly and dangerously. It produces hydrogen gas and so much heat that it can cause the hydrogen to catch alight. Some materials react quicker and release more heat than others when they react with substances such as water and oxygen. We can compare and choose materials for use based on their ability to react called **reactivity**. For example, we use unreactive metals such as gold for jewellery because it does not react with oxygen in air or chemicals in sweat that could change its appearance.

Eureka!

In 1777 French scientist Antoine-Laurent Lavoisier discovered that burning was caused by materials reacting with oxygen, releasing lots of heat in the process.

Prosthetic legs are often made from light, strong alloys of metals such as titanium. Such metals have low reactivity so the leg can be worn in any conditions without reacting.

Try this!

During any chemical reaction the atoms in materials rearrange but do not disappear. Demonstrate this using the reaction between vinegar and baking soda.

Prediction

The weight of materials after a chemical reaction is the same as the weight before the reaction even though the type of material has changed.

Equipment

- 2 plastic cups
- 1 large zip lock bag that can easily hold the 2 cups
- 500 ml (1 pint) vinegar solution (also called acetic acid)
- pack or tin of baking soda (also called sodium bicarbonate)
- electronic scales with a large weighing area
- pencil and paper

Be safe!

Safety goggles and aprons must be worn during this demonstration to prevent being splashed by the fizzing!

Method

① Fill one cup halfway with vinegar.

② Fill the second cup halfway with baking soda.

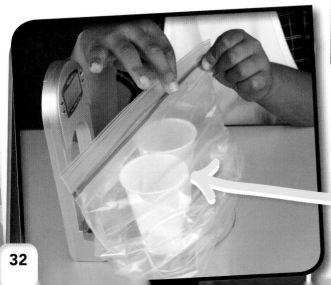

③ Open the bag and rest on the scales. Carefully put both cups in the plastic bag. Take care NOT to spill the contents of either cup.

4 Measure and record the total weight of the cups, their contents and the plastic bag.

5 Seal the plastic bag completely. Otherwise substances formed during the reaction could spray out.

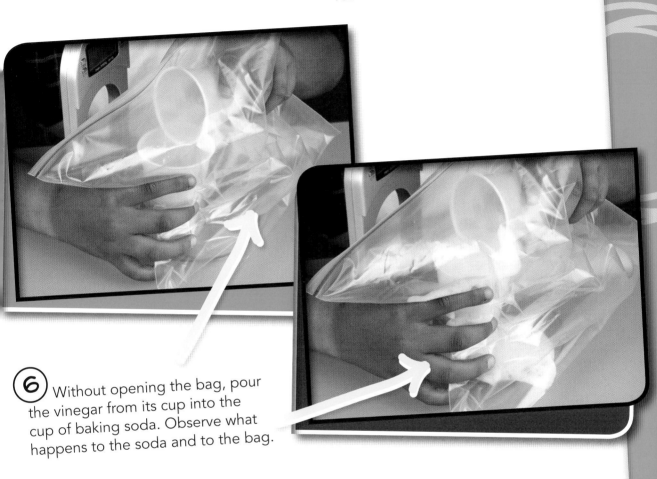

6 Without opening the bag, pour the vinegar from its cup into the cup of baking soda. Observe what happens to the soda and to the bag.

7 Without opening the bag, weigh and record the total weight of the plastic bag and its contents. Was it the same as in step 4?

Results

Baking soda and vinegar react to form carbon dioxide gas and other substances. The gas bubbles through the mixture and inflates the bag as it takes up more space than the starting substances. You should find that the total weight stays the same because all the substances formed during the reaction – including carbon dioxide – were trapped in the bag.

What new materials do we make?

Take a walk through your home, school, village, or city and imagine a world without glass, concrete, or plastic. People make these materials they need from raw materials using a variety of chemical changes.

Glass

The main raw material used to make glass is sand, which is mined from sand dunes, beaches, underground, or underwater. Sand is heated with ground-up limestone and the sticky substance formed is rolled or pressed into shape before cooling. The melted sand reacts with the limestone to make glass less brittle than using sand alone. A material called soda ash is added to the mix to lower the melting point of sand, which means that less energy is used to make the glass. Other chemicals are added to make coloured glass or glass containers that can survive higher temperatures.

Melted or molten glass is hot and soft. People can blow into the glass through tubes to stretch the glass into hollow shapes that harden as they cool.

Tougher glass

Drinking glasses break easily when dropped onto a hard floor and windows can shatter if a football or stone hits them. In factories people can make toughened glass by heating glass to high temperatures then cooling and pressing it rapidly. Another tough substance called glass-reinforced plastic or fibreglass is made of thin fibres of glass held together in strong glue. This can be formed into many different shapes, from boats to hot tubs.

Toughened glass is up to five times stronger than ordinary glass. That means that it is much harder to break.

DID YOU KNOW?

Some volcanoes produce natural black glass when very sticky, hot molten rock containing lots of silica and very little water erupts and suddenly cools. The glass is called obsidian and is sometimes used for jewellery.

Concrete

Concrete is the major building material in the world because it is as strong as stone but cheaper and more adaptable. It is made as a liquid that can be poured into a mould where it sets in any shape. Blocks of concrete can be attached together to form walls and columns in buildings.

Concrete is made by mixing together crushed stone, sand, water, and cement. Cement is a grey powder made by heating and grinding limestone with clay and gypsum. Concrete forms when the cement reacts with water to set hard around the stone or sand, which gives it bulk. This material is very strong but can be made stronger and less likely to break by supporting the concrete with steel wire or mesh.

DID YOU KNOW?

Around 7 billion cubic metres (250 billion cubic feet) of concrete are produced each year worldwide to build structures with. That is about 1 cubic metre (35 cubic feet) for each human on the planet.

Before pouring concrete foundations, steel mesh is wired together into a tough skeleton for the concrete to harden and set around, making a very strong and rigid structure.

The trouble with concrete

Carbon dioxide is released during the manufacture and use of concrete. This gas is a **greenhouse gas** that stores heat in the atmosphere, causing worldwide changes in temperature called **global warming**. The cement and concrete industry produces 5 per cent of all the man-made carbon dioxide released into the atmosphere.

Eureka!

In 1824 English bricklayer Joseph Aspdin first made Portland cement by burning powdered limestone and clay in his kitchen stove. He named it after a type of stone from Portland in Dorset, UK because it looked similar to that. It is now the basic ingredient for most concrete.

Concrete is often used to stick bricks made from hardened clay together into vertical walls.

Making plastics

Most plastics are made from oil, which is a mixture of substances. Oil is heated to separate the different substances such as ethene. To make poly(ethene) or polythene, for example, chemical reactions are carried out to make ethene molecules join together, like many paper clips forming longer chains. This makes the longer molecules of poly(ethene). Further reactions join polyethene with chlorine to make polyethene chloride, or PVC.

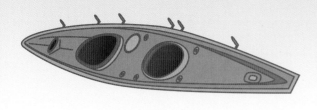

The kayak mould is made from smooth metal

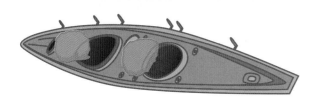

Powdered polyethylene of any colour is poured into the bottom half of the mould and the top half is clamped on

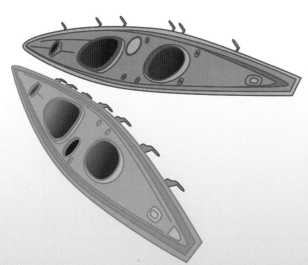

The complete mould is put into a special hot oven to melt the plastic. It is rocked and rolled to spread the plastic around. The mould is removed from the oven, slowly cooled, and the halves separated to reveal a kayak!

Soft, melted plastic can be made into different shapes. It can be pressed through holes or slits to make anything from sheets to threads. It can be squirted into **moulds** to make objects such as boats or toys, and have air blown through it to make hollow shapes such as bottles.

Green plastic

One of the useful properties of plastic is that it does not rot easily. However, this becomes a problem when plastic objects are thrown away because they build up in waste dumps. People can create long molecules to make plastics from plants such as maize and peas, wood, and plant oils. These molecules break down more easily than those from oil.

WHAT'S NEXT?

In future, people plan to grow plastics similar to polystyrene from crop waste using mushrooms. Plastic grows as the mushrooms absorb nutrients from the waste!

These are reuseable polycarbonate milk bottles made in moulds. Polycarbonate is very strong, transparent and resistant to high temperatures. This means that the empty milk bottles can be washed at temperatures high enough to kill any bacteria before refilling with milk.

Try this!

A bouncy ball needs to be elastic and strong so it jumps up and does not break when dropped onto a hard surface. You can make your own using glue!

Prediction

A chemical reaction with other materials changes glue and cornstarch into a bouncy ball.

Equipment

- clear or white all purpose glue
- borax powder (available from DIY stores and chemists)
- Cornstarch or cornflour
- 2 plastic cups
- 2 wooden craft sticks or drink stirrers
- teaspoon and tablespoon
- food colouring of the colour you want your ball to be
- small sealing food bag

Method

(1) Put 1 tablespoon of glue and 5 drops of food colouring into one of the plastic cups. Mix with one of the sticks or stirrers. Add more colouring if the glue colour is too light.

(2) Make a borax solution by stirring one teaspoon of borax powder into two tablespoons of warm tap water in the second cup. TAKE CARE WHEN USING HOT WATER.

(3) WITHOUT MIXING add one tablespoon of cornstarch and half a teaspoon of borax solution to the glue. Leave for 15 seconds.

4 Then stir the mixture until it becomes sticky and thick.

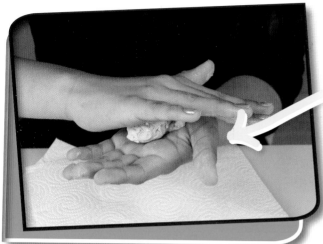

5 Now the messy bit: pick up the mixture and mould it in your hands. It will become more solid as you roll it in your hands into a ball shape.

6 Have fun bouncing your ball on a hard floor somewhere where it cannot cause damage. Store it in the food bag when not in use to stop it drying out and crumbling.

Be safe!
Wash your hands after mixing and after playing with the ball and never eat any of the materials used to make the ball or the ball itself.

Results
The glue contains a strong and flexible plastic that gives the ball strength. The cornstarch gives the ball elasticity. The borax makes the glue and the starch stick together while the ball is being bounced!

How do we choose materials?

People have a wide choice of materials to make the things they need. The actual ones they use depends partly on properties and cost. For example, wood makes very buoyant, tough and attractive ocean yachts. However, this material can rot in seawater or get eaten by sea worms unless the boat is painted or varnished regularly! Plastic boats are easier and cheaper to care for or maintain than wooden ones. People also choose materials based on their impact on the planet. Sustainable development is when we continue to use resources to meet our needs but preserve the environment while doing so.

DID YOU KNOW?

A rare material called coltan is used to make the small electrical parts in mobile phones work. The problem is that coltan is only found in central Africa. It is in such demand that people are chopping down rainforests to mine it, and miners are killing rare forest animals to eat, including gorillas.

Many machines use a combination of materials chosen for their different properties. What different materials can you spot on this all-terrain vehicle?

Sustainable development

Some material use is unsustainable. For example, making garden furniture from rainforest trees is often cheap, but as rainforests disappear there is less space and less food for wildlife and people that live there. So, many people choose furniture made from timber grown in carefully managed forests. In these new trees are planted to replace those that are cut down. This is more expensive but causes less damage. Some people prefer to choose things made from renewable materials such as **recycled** metal made by melting down used metal.

WHAT'S NEXT?

China is planning to fly spacecraft to the moon and use robots to mine materials that are common there but much rarer on Earth, such as fuel used in nuclear reactors!

In sustainable forestry new trees are planted after mature ones are harvested. In the best sustainable woodlands there is a mixture of tree types that provide habitats for a wide variety of living things, the trees are cared for, and the soil is conserved to make sure of future harvests.

Glossary

alloy mixture of two or more metals with a combination of their individual properties

aluminium type of light, soft metal used to make anything from drinks cans and cooking foil to aircraft parts

atom tiny particle of matter. Every material and living thing is made from atoms.

boiling point temperature at which a liquid changes to a gas

bond joining force between two atoms or molecules

buoyancy ability of an object or material to float in water or other materials

carbon type of matter making up materials such as oil, coal, diamond, carbon dioxide gas, and living things

chemical reaction when materials combine to produce new materials with different properties

condensation change of state from gas to liquid

conductor material that heat or electricity moves through easily, such as metal

copper type of metal that is a good conductor of electricity and used in electrical wires

density property of a material that represents its mass for every unit of its volume. For example, lead has a higher density than polystyrene

dissolve mix completely with a liquid. For example, salt and sugar dissolve in water

erosion process in which pieces of materials are carried away by moving water, wind, or other forces

evaporate change of state from liquid to gas. Liquids evaporate when heat or moving air gives their molecules enough energy to escape the liquid

flammable something that catches fire easily

fossil fuel material including oil, coal, and gas. These formed underground over millions of years from remains of ancient organisms

freezing point temperature at which a liquid becomes a solid

fuel substance that contains and releases lots of energy, usually as heat

global warming gradual rise in global temperatures caused by the build-up of gases in the atmosphere such as carbon dioxide, released by machines and factories

gypsum type of mineral found underground or in soil that is used for example to make concrete and plaster

insulator material such as plastic that does not conduct heat or electricity well

iron strong and magnetic metal used to make steel

irreversible change that cannot be reversed, such as cooking an omelette. Cooling the omelette does not turn it back into runny eggs again!

limestone type of rock that formed from tiny pieces of sand, mud or shells, useful in making concrete and glass

melting point temperature at which a solid changes into a liquid

molecule particle made from two or more atoms joined together

mould container that holds a liquid or soft solid that sets into its shape

non-renewable natural material that cannot be replaced once it is used up, such as coal

product substance formed during a chemical reaction

property feature or characteristic of something that can affect how a material behaves in different conditions

raw material natural substance such as oil or wood that can be made into other useful materials

reactivity ability of a substance to react

recycle change used materials into new products, for example used plastic drink bottles into a fleece

renewable natural material that can be replaced as it is used up, such as wood

reversible change that can go forwards or backwards, such as melting ice into water and freezing the water

silicon type of substance found in sand and other materials useful for making solar cells and glass

solute substance that dissolves in a solvent

solution mixture in which one or more substances are dissolved in another

solvent liquid in which another substance dissolves

vibrate shake or jiggle around

weathering process of gradual breakdown of rock, soil and other materials for example by changes in temperature

Find out more

Books

Amazing Materials (Amazing Science), Sally Hewitt (Crabtree, 2007)

Materials (Go Facts: Physical Science), Ian Rohr (A&C Black, 2009)

The Reactions of Metals (Sci-Hi), Roberta Baxter (Raintree, 2009)

The Story Behind Plastic (True Stories), Christin Ditchfield (Raintree, 2012)

Websites

classroom.materials.ac.uk/index.php
Explore what materials go into an mp3 player or a car, and take a quiz on materials at this great website. You can even play a game called Scan-bot where a robot moves through a house identifying materials!

www.acs.org
Learn more about chemical and physical changes, the characteristics of materials, and other science topics in the Science or Kids section of the Education menu of the main page.

www.explainthatstuff.com/articles_materials.html
Find out some interesting details about a wide range of materials.

www.materials-careers.org.uk
Visit this site to discover more about understanding and using materials, and how knowledge of materials is useful for a range of different careers.

www.sciencemuseum.org.uk/onlinestuff/stories/materials_of_the_future.aspx
Want to learn about some of the materials of the future? Go to this Science Museum site to find out more.

Places to visit

Visit the Challenge of Material gallery at the Science Museum in South Kensington, London, to see a wide range of objects made of different materials, and learn about the history and future of materials.

Go to the Matter Factory at The Children's Museum of Houston, Texas, USA, to explore how molecules and atoms make up materials, investigate materials and learn about smart materials.

At the Exploratorium in San Francisco, USA, you can have an exciting, hands-on experience learning about materials in The World of Matter space and all sorts of science topics.

Further research

Bamboo is a very fast-growing, tough member of the grass family. Find out more about this renewable material, where it grows, and its uses.

What is the history of concrete? Here is a clue: the Pantheon in Rome.

Discover some of the different materials developed for the space programme since the 1960s, especially in the USA, such as space blankets, cooling suits, and visors.

Find pictures of houses and other buildings worldwide made from recycled materials.

Index